# Nutrition recommendations during TCM - Stomach - Yin Deficiency

Please check these recommendations always with a nutrition consultant, therapist, doctor or dietician. The recipes and the list of ingredients are supporting the conventional medical therapy. The calorie disclosures of fresh ingredients (fruit and vegetables) vary according to quality and time of harvest. The contents were checked by a dietician and a nutrition consultant for the Traditional Chinese Medicine (TCM).

Author:
©2020 Josef Miligui
www.ebns.at

AF285135

Source:
The lists are created from the EBNS database for nutritional counseling. The database is used by dietitians, therapists and doctors for advising the patient / client.

Literature:
The specialist literature and the training documents of the German and Austrian dietary and traditional Chinese medicine serve as a knowledge base. We have used the documents as a basis of knowledge, adapted it to our experience and completed them.
http://nutribook.info/

Production and publishing:
BoD – Books on Demand, Norderstedt
ISBN: 9783752894042

# Nutrition recommendations for TCM - Stomach - Yin Deficiency

# 1   Treatment strategy

Strengthen stomach yin, nourish body fluids, strengthen middle over spleen build QI.
Hot NO, warm LITTLE (sour and bitter NO), neutral and refreshing YES

# 2   Avoid

Bitter or dehydrating food and drink, coffee, red wine, green tea, black tea, cigarettes, grilled, roasted and smoked foods, spicy hot spices, brandy, vinegar.

# 3   Breakfast

|  | kkal. per serving |
|---|---|
| Cooling rice dish with grapefruit | 234 |
| Polenta with ratatouille | 225 |
| Tea from celery sticks | 0,7 |
| Tea from licorice (heart-strengthening) | 19 |
| Tea from mallow | 0 |
| Tea from marshmallow tea | 0 |

# 4   Snack

| Polenta with ratatouille | 225 |
|---|---|

# 5   Lunch

| 8 treasures of rice | 212 |
|---|---|
| Artichoke soup | 142 |
| Beetroot soup | 282 |
| Carp soup | 166 |
| Chicken soup with angelica root and buckthorn fruit | 77 |
| Cooling rice dish with grapefruit | 234 |
| Polenta with ratatouille | 225 |
| Tea from celery sticks | 0,7 |
| Tea from licorice (heart-strengthening) | 19 |
| Tea from mallow | 0 |
| Tea from marshmallow tea | 0 |

# 6   Afternoon

n.a.

# 7 Dinner

# 8 Any time

# 9 Recipes

(rec.) = You can use more.
(little) = You should use less than specified
(omit) = omit.

## 9.1 8 treasures of rice

Strengthens kidney and bladder, builds up Qi, strengthens the spleen, repels moisture, reduces internal heat, prevents cancer, builds heart, calms nerves.
Cooking time approx. 1 hour
Calories p. portion: 212
4 portions

**Quantity of ingredients**
Lily bulbs 1 table spoon / 5g. () - cool - sweet, bitter ........................................ *
Longane 1 table spoon / 5g. (little) - warm - sweet............................................ *
King Solomon's-seal 1 table spoon / 5g. () - neutral - sweet, bitter .................. *
Yam root, yam root tuber 1 table spoon / 5g. () - neutral - sweet ..................... *
Coix (seeds) YiYi Ren 1 table spoon / 5g. () - cool - sweet, neutral ................. *
Rice wild (nature rice) 1 1/2 cups / 240g. () - neutral - sweet, bitter .......... metal
Water 8-10 cups / 800g. (yes) - cool - salty................................................earth

**Cooking instructions:**
Each one 1 tbsp: Bai He, Longan, Yu Zhu, Da Zao, Shan Yao, Lian Mi, Yi Yi Ren, Qian Shi
Add hot water and soak for about 30 minutes. Then add 1 - 2 cups of rice (normal) and simmer for 1/2 to 1 hour until the rice is very soft. Or: Cook for about 3 hours with the herbs a congee. Then the herbs do not have to be soaked.

## 9.2   Artichoke soup

Cools heat, nourishes heart, stomach and lungs Yin.
Cooking time approx. 40 min
Calories p. portion: 143
3 portions
Allergens: GLN

### Quantity of ingredients
Artichoke 4 pieces / 400g. (yes) - cool - sweet, bitter .................................... fire
Butter organic 1 table spoon / 20g. (rec.) - neutral - sweet ......................... earth
Onion (shallot) 1 piece / 20g. (little) - warm - acrid, sweet ........................ metal
Corn flour 1 table spoon / 10g. () - neutral - sweet .................................... earth
Nutmeg 1 pinch / 0,5g. () - warm - acrid ..................................................... metal
Basic recipe for a vegetable soup (nutritious) 1 cup / 250g. (rec.) - neutral - *. *
Salt 1 pinch / 0,5g. (little) - cold - salty ..................................................... water
Lemon 1/4 piece / 8g. () - cold - sour ......................................................... wood
Lemon peel 1/4 piece / 1g. (little) - cool - bitter ............................................ fire
Turmeric (yellow root) 1 pinch / 1g. (yes) - warm - bitter ................................. *
Sesame, white 1 teaspoon / 10g. (yes) - neutral - sweet ............................ earth

### Cooking instructions:
Boil the artichokes in 2 liters of water with salt until the outer leaves are
light removable. Remove leaves and flower center (fibrous) so that only
the soil remains.
Melt the butter, cut the onion into small pieces and steam gently; add
some cornmeal, nutmeg; brew with vegetable soup; add salt, a little
lemon peel and juice, turmeric and artichoke bottoms, cook gently and
puree; Season with Tahin and sprinkle with sesame before serving.


## 9.3   Beetroot soup

Dissolves stagnation, relaxes, builds up Qi.
Cooking time approx. 20-30 min
Calories p. portion: 282
4 portions
Allergens: G

### Quantity of ingredients
Olive oil 2 table spoons / 20g. (rec.) - cool - sweet .................................... earth
Onion white 1 piece chopped / 50g. (little) - warm - acrid .......................... metal
Garlic 1 clove / 2g. () - hot - acrid .............................................................. metal

Red beet 2,2 lbs (Peeled and diced) / 1000g. () - neutral - bitter................earth
Cumin (Caraway seed) 1 table spoon / 7g. (little) - warm - acrid...............metal
Curcuma 1 teaspoon / 2g. () - warm - bitter...................................................... *
Oregano fresh 1 pinch of fresh / 2g. () - warm - bitter ...............................metal
Peppers (rose peppers) 1 teaspoon / 2g. () - warm - bitter.........................earth
Créme fraiche cheese 1/4 lbs - 4oz / 125g. (yes) - neutral - sweet ...........earth

## Cooking instructions:

Heat the oil in a saucepan, fry the onions and garlic in dark brown. Add cumin, turmeric, oregano and salt and deglaze with 1 liter of water. Cook the beetroot for about 20 minutes. Puree the soup and serve in soup bowls with 1 tbsp. creme fraiche. Finally, sprinkle the rose pepper over it.

## 9.4   Carp soup

Nourishing and slightly warming, strengthens the middle and the lower heater, removes moisture.
Cooking time approx. 2 hours
Calories p. portion: 166
6 portions
Allergens: DO

## Quantity of ingredients

Carp 1,1 lbs / 500g. (yes) - neutral - salty ................................................water
Salt 1 pinch / 1g. (little) - cold - salty .......................................................water
Vinegar (Apple vinegar) 1 teaspoon / 3g. () - warm - sour, bitter.............wood
Thyme 1 Twig / 3g. (little) - warm - bitter...................................................... *
Juniper berry 8 pieces / 3g. () - warm - sweet, acrid, bitter...........................fire
Carrot 2 pieces / 200g. (rec.) - neutral - sweet...........................................earth
Leek 1 piece / 200g. (little) - warm - acrid .................................................metal
Onion white 1 piece / 60g. (little) - warm - acrid .......................................metal
Ginger fresh 1/2 teaspoon / 2g. (little) - warm - acrid ...............................metal
Bay leaf 3 leaves / 1g. () - warm - acrid.......................................................... *
White wine 1/2 cup / 125g. () - cool - sweet, bitter, acrid..........................wood
Basil 3 leaves / 1g. (yes) - warm - acrid, bitter ...............................................fire
Water 4 cup / 800g. (yes) - cool - salty.......................................................earth

## Cooking instructions:

Preparation: When shopping at the fishmonger, remove the fillets from a medium-sized, whole carp and also pack the fish head, spine with bones and tail.

Cut the fillets into 1 cm cubes; salt and set aside.

Place fish head, backbone and tail of carp in plenty of cold water; heat till it boils and scoop the foam; add a dash of vinegar, a fresh sprig of thyme, juniper berries; Add carrot, a piece of leek and chopped onion; add a thick slice of ginger, some peppercorns, 1 bay leaf, salt; simmer for about 1 1/2 hours and pour the stock through a sieve.

Put the carp pieces in a saucepan; pour a shot of white wine; Add rose paprika, basil leaves, finely ground carrots, dried thyme and the stock and warm; Boil the ingredients for about 5 minutes until the fish pieces are cooked.
Variants: Thicken the soup with kuzu or mashed potatoes.
This fits: baguette and dry white wine.

## 9.5   Chicken soup with angelica root and buckthorn fruit

Strengthens spleen and nourishes the blood and Yin of the liver, forces Qi and blood, is very warming.
Cooking time approx. 1 1/2 hours
Calories p. portion: 77
3 portions
Allergens: LO

### Quantity of ingredients
Basic recipe for a chicken soup (warming) 2 cup / 500g. () - warm - * ............. *
Bocksdorn fruits (Fructus Lycii, Goji 1/8 lbs - 2oz / 50g. () - cool - ........... wood

### Cooking instructions:
When you cook chicken broth according to basic recipes add angelica root and willowberry fruits in the last 40 minutes.

Ingestion: Drink 2-3 cups of broth daily.

## 9.6   Cooling rice dish with grapefruit

Lowers lung Qi, nourishes fluids, dissolves mucus, dries out, passes downwardly, warms the stomach and spleen, harmonizes the intestine, forces Qi, reduces moisture, strengthens Qi and Kidney Jing, moisturizes, relaxes, builds up Qi, spreads.
Cooking time approx. 20 min
Calories p. portion: 234
4 portions
Allergens: GHO

**Quantity of ingredients**
Rice round grain 1 cup / 120g. () - neutral - sweet ................................... metal
Water 5 cups / 600g. (yes) - cool - salty ..................................... earth
Hazelnuts 2 table spoons / 20g. (yes) - neutral - sweet ............................ earth
Raisins 2 table spoons / 20g. (little) - warm - sweet ................................... earth
Agave nectar 1 table spoon / 10g. () - cool - sweet ......................................... *
Salt 1 pinch / 0,2g. (little) - cold - salty ...................................... water
Almond puree 1 table spoon / 10g. (rec.) - neutral - sweet.......................... earth
Grapefruit (Pomelo) 1 piece / 200g. () - cool - sweet, sour............................ fire
Butter organic 2 teaspoons / 20g. (rec.) - neutral - sweet .......................... earth

**Cooking instructions:**
Preparation on the eve: Pour round grain rice into cold water and cook. Soak chopped hazelnuts and raisins in some hot water overnight.

In the morning: Stir in a little hot water some agave syrup; add the rice and heat; add a small pinch of salt, almond paste, chopped grapefruit, the soaked chopped hazelnuts and raisins and mix; Serve with a small piece of butter.

## 9.7   Polenta with ratatouille

Strengthens stomach Qi, diuretic, moisturizes, relaxes, builds up Qi, spreads, nourishes liver-Yin, cools heat, produces humors, cools and moves blood, reduces external and internal wind, reduces internal heat.
Cooking time approx. 30 min
Calories p. portion: 226
4 portions
Allergens: G

**Quantity of ingredients**

Corn Grease (Polenta) 1 cup / 120g. (rec.) - neutral - sweet......................earth
Water 1 1/2 cups / 240g. (yes) - cool - salty...............................................earth
Aubergine 1 piece (large) / 200g. (yes) - cool - sweet...............................earth
Zucchini 2 pieces / 500g. (rec.) - cool - sweet...........................................earth
Onion white 2 pieces / 120g. (little) - warm - acrid ....................................metal
Tomato 2 pieces (blended) / 200g. (rec.) - cold - sweet-sour ....................wood
Olive oil 2 table spoons / 20g. (rec.) - cool - sweet....................................earth
Salt 1 pinch / 0,5g. (little) - cold - salty .....................................................water
Parsley 1 table spoon (chopped) / 8g. (yes) - warm - bitter.......................wood
Thyme 1/2 teaspoon / 1g. (little) - warm - bitter................................................ *
Onion spring 2 table spoons (chopped) / 12g. (little) - warm - acrid ..........metal
Basil 4 leaves / 2g. (yes) - warm - acrid, bitter ..............................................fire

**Cooking instructions:**

Use double the amount of water to polenta, add salt and oil and heat till it boils. Stir in polenta, stirring constantly. Take off the fire and let it swell for 20 minutes. Meanwhile, cut the onion, fry in a saucepan with hot oil. Add the diced zucchini, tomatoes and melanzani and simmer for about 20 minutes. Add basil, thyme, salt.
Coat baking tray with oil, apply polenta evenly and wait until it gets stronger.
Add the cooked ratatouille to polenta, portion and then put in the oven for a few minutes (possibly with grated parmesan).
Sprinkle with fresh parsley and finely chopped spring onion.
The valuable tip: The Polenta sections are ideal for on the go.

# 9.8   Tea from celery sticks

Brings the Liver Qi in motion, cools heat, moisturizes, relaxes, builds up Qi, spreads.
Cooking time approx. 15 min
Calories p. portion: 1
4 portions
Allergens: L

**Quantity of ingredients**

Celery sticks 2 table spoons (chopped) / 18g. (rec.) - cool - sweet ............earth
Water 2 cup / 500g. (yes) - cool - salty.......................................................earth

**Cooking instructions:**

Heat the water till it boils and put it aside. Add cutted celery and cook for 10 min. to let go. Strain. Sweet to taste with honey.

## 9.9 Tea from licorice (heart-strengthening)

Strengthen spleen and stomach Qi, nourishes Yin from heart and kidney, moisturizes, forces heart and kidney, reduces internal heat, preserves the fluids, contracts.
Cooking time approx. 15 min
Calories p. portion: 20
4 portions

### Quantity of ingredients
Dates red 2 table spoons (chopped) / 20g. () - warm - sweet.....................earth
Wheat 2 teaspoons (milled) / 16g. (rec.) - cool - sweet ............................ wood
Water 2 cup / 500g. (yes) - cool - salty......................................................earth

### Cooking instructions:
Simmer licorice root, red dates and wheat for 40 minutes, strain and keep the tea in the refrigerator. Throw away the ingredients.
Variant: This recipe can be supplemented with chicken broth; it will be even stronger.
Decoction: 2-4 teaspoons, sprinkle licorice with 1/2 liter of cold water, heat till it boils, cook for 1 min, leave for 10 min. Drink 1 cup twice a day.

## 9.10 Tea from mallow

Preserves the fluids, contracts, cools liver fire, forces stomach-Yin. Dissolves mucus of the pores of the heart.
Cooking time approx. 10 min
Calories p. portion: 0
4 portions

### Quantity of ingredients
Mallow (Malva sylvestris) blossom tea 2 teabags / 4g. (rec.) - cool - sour ....... *
Water 2 cup / 500g. (yes) - cool - salty......................................................earth

### Cooking instructions:
Heat the water till it boils and put it aside. Add mallow tee and 10 min. to let go. Sweet to taste with honey. Strain when pouring.

# 10 Effects of food

## 10.1 Use ingredients: recommendable

Almond marzipan
Almond milk
Almond puree
Basic recipe for a duck soup
Basic recipe for a fish soup
Basic recipe for a vegetable soup
(nutritious)
Beef stomach
Black beans
Broad beans (thick beans)
Butter organic
Carrot
Carrot (Early Carrot)
Carrot juice without sugar
Celery sticks
Champignon
Chard
Chicken stomach
Chicken yolk
Chinese cabbage
Coconut flakes
Coconut grated
Corn Grease (Polenta)
Cress
Crucian
Cucumber
Dill
Duck (slaughtered)
Fig
Fig dried
Fresh cheese
Hibiscus
Licorice root tea
Linseed oil
Mallow (Malva sylvestris) blossom tea
Malt
Mung bean sprouting
Olive oil
Oyster mushroom
Peanut oil
Pear

Pear juice
Pine nuts
Pistachios
Pork meat
Pork stomach
Pumpkin seeds
Quail egg
Rabbit liver
Rabbit meat
Rapeseed oil
Reishi mushroom
Rice Basmati
Rice long grain rice
Rose leaf tea
Saffron
Salsify
Sesame oil
Soy Tofu
Soybeans, black
Spinach
Sugar cane sugar
Sugar fructose - fruit sugar
Sugar glucose - grapes sugar
Sugar Milk Sugar
Sugar molasses
Sunflower seeds
Sweet potato
Thistle oil
Tomato
Vanilla
Vanilla powder
Watermelon
Wheat
Wheat flakes
Wheat semolina
Wheat semolina for children
Yogurt (natural, 1.5% fat)
Yogurt (natural, 3.5% fat)
Zucchini

# 10.2 Use ingredients: yes

Adzuki beans
Apple (sweet)
Apple juice (natural cloudy)
Arrowroot
Artichoke
Aubergine
Basic recipe for a rice soup (Congee)
Basil
Basil (fresh)
Beef liver
Bitter melon
Blackberry´s
Boletus mushroom
Borage
Breadcrumbs (wheat bread, bread roll)
Broccoli
Brussels sprouts
Calamari
Cantaloupe
Carp
Cashews
Cauliflower
Celery root
Chanterelle
Chervil
Chestnuts
Chicken egg
Chickpeas
Chicory
Chlorella (fresh water)
Corn
Couscous
Cow's milk (1.5% fat)
Cow's milk (whole milk 3.5% fat)
Créme fraiche cheese
Elderberry blossom tee
Fennel
Fennel seeds ground
Fish pieces mixed (fresh water)
Freshwater fish
Gourd
Grape juice red
Grape juice white
Grapes red
Grapes white
Ground caraway
Hawthorn
Hazelnuts
Herbs various
Honey
Lentils

Lentils black
Lentils red
Lentils yellow
Lychee
Lychee in Preserved
Margarine
Margarine (diet)
Morel, dried
Mozzarella
Mulberry fruit
Multi-grain bread (gray bread)
Mung bean
Octopus
Okra
Olives
Oregano dried
Papaya
Parmesan
Parsley
Parsley root
Parsnip
Peanuts
Peas
Peas, green
Peppers
Perch
Pork heart
Pork knuckle
Pork liver
Pork skin
Potato
Pumpkin
Quail
Quince
Quinoa
Radish black
Red cabbage
Rice (whole grain)
Rice flour
Rice malt
Rice noodles
Rice variety any
Rye
Rye flour
Sage
Salmon
Savory
Sesame paste (Tahini)
Sesame, black
Sesame, white
Shiitake, dried

Soybean milk
Soybeans, yellow
Sunflower oil
Tarragon (Estragon)
Trout
Turmeric (yellow root)
Water
Water hot
Wheat flour
Wheat germ oil
White bread (wheat bread)

# 10.3 Use ingredients: little

Agar agar (kelp)
Anchovy / Sardine
Anise (Common Fennel)
Apricot
Apricots
Avocado
Balm
Banana
Banana (cooking banana)
Beef fillet
Beef meat
Beef meat (calf)
Beef meatbones
Black caraway
Black-eyed peas
Blueberry
Blueberry juice
Cherry
Cherry juice
Chives
Clove
Coconut milk
Cod
Coriander
Cumin (Caraway seed)
Currant (black)
Currant (red)
Currant (white)
Deer meat
French beans
Ginger fresh
Gooseberry
Grass carp
Ground
Herring
Kohlrabi
Kombu seaweed (Saccharina japonica)
Kumquats
Lamb bones
Lamb meat
Lamb shoulder
Leek
Lemon peel
Lobster
Longane
Mackerel

Marjoram
Mediterranean fish (cod, plaice,
haddock, sea eel, mackerel)
Mullet
Mustard seeds
Oat
Oat flakes (whole grain)
Oat flour
Oat fusion (baby food)
Onion (shallot)
Onion (spring onion)
Onion read
Onion white
Pepper Cayenne
Pepper white (ground)
Peppercorns
Pheasant
Pigeon
Plaice
Pomegranate
Raisins
Raspberry
Raspberry dried (immature)
Rice (fragrance)
Rosefish
Sago (cereals)
Salt
Shark
Sour milk cheese 20%
Soybean oil
Spiny lobsters
Star anise
Strawberries
Strawberry Juice
Sugar brown
Sugar candy white
Sugar white
Thyme
Tuna
Wakame
Walnuts
Wheat beer
Wheat bulgur
Wild boar meat

## 10.4 Do not use contra-acting foods

Apple (sour)
Asparagus (green or white)
Black tea
Buckwheat (roasted) Kasha
Burdock root tea
Caviar
Cereal coffee
Chicken liver
Chili (pod or ground)
Chocolate
Cinnamon ground
Cinnamon sticks
Clementines
Cocoa
Coffee
Crab
Cranberry
Cranberry juice
Cream, sweet 30%
Curcuma
Curd cheese 20%
Curd cheese 40%
Curry
Dandelion (young plants)
Deer meat
Feta cheese
Garlic
Ginger powder
Goat
Goat and sheep's milk
Goat cheese
Green spelt
Green tea
Hyssop
Juniper berry
Kefir
Kiwi
Lemon
Lemon juice
Lime
Lovage
Mango

Millet
Millet flakes
Miso paste (soy bean paste)
Mold cheese
Mussels
Mutton
Nutmeg
Orange
Orange juice
Peaches
Peaches (canned)
Peppers (rose peppers)
Pickle
Pimento
Pineapple
Pineapple (from a can)
Pineapple juice without sugar
Plum
Poppy
Radish (white, green, purple-red)
Red wine
Rhubarb
Rose hip tea
Rosemary
Sake
Sauerkraut (cutted cabbage fermented)
Seacrab
Sorrel
Sour cherries
Sour cream 15% fat
Sour milk
Soy sauce
Spirit
Tangerine
Umeboshi plums (Japanese apricots)
Vinegar (Apple vinegar)
Vinegar (Red wine vinegar)
Vinegar Aceto Balsamico
Wheat bran
White wine
Yogi tea

# 11 Complementary

## 11.1 Ginseng root

Panax notoginseng, Radix
Preparation: Decoction
Build up origin-Qi, build spleen, moisturize lungs, produce essence.
Tonifies stomach-yin.

Drink 5-10 g in one dose in the morning on an empty stomach
For a tincture, draw 50-60 g of high quality ginseng in 1 liter of alcohol for
2-4 months, then take 25-30 ml once or twice daily on an empty stomach.

In animal studies with aflatoxin-induced cancer animals show that
ginseng was 75% less likely to have liver cancer and 29% less likely to
develop lung cancer than animals that did not get ginseng. Several times,
ginseng proved beneficial in animal studies on lung cancer. Ginseng was
also active against human ovarian cancer cells implanted in animals and
protected mice from liver cancer.

According to a Korean study with 1987 participants, the regular intake of
Panax ginseng could halve the risk of cancer depending on the type of
cancer (although, unfortunately, there was no such link between breast
cancer, cervical cancer, bladder cancer and thyroid cancer). People who
ate ginseng for one year had a 36% lower cancer risk. At the age of 5
years, the cancer rate was even 69% lower.

As you can see, both healthy and cancer patients can benefit from
ginseng, but costs are a significant factor. In addition, the rather
inconsistent standards of purity and strength require the consumer to do
some research.

Do not use: together with radish and tea, colds, pneumonia or other lung
infections, incompatibility with: Iron or other metal components, amethyst,
dairy products.

## 11.2 Hibiscus

Althaea
Preparation: Healing tea (infusion)
Nourishes Kidney-Yin and Lung-Yin, Derives Void-Heat, Nourishes
Stomach-Yin, Cooling, Moisturizing.
Active ingredients: cane sugar, pectin, many minerals

# 12 Basics of Nutrition

The basic principles of nutrition described herein are general
recommendations. They are not aimed at a specific form of therapy.
Recommendations concerning a therapy have priority.

## 12.1 Nutrition

Regular meals in a relaxed atmosphere. A warm breakfast is considered
a good start into the day.
The main meals ought to be taken for lunch – supper in the early
evening. Pay attention to feeling hungry or sated: don't eat too much nor
remain hungry is the rule
Prepare the meals freshly from natural, regional products. Frozen, heat-
conserved, industrially prepared or foodstuffs cooked in the microwave
oven are rejected.
Choice of foodstuffs according to the season: more cooling food in
summer, more warming food in winter.
Eat cooked food at least twice a day. Food and drinks ought to be
lukewarm, never ice-cold or hot.
Raw vegetables, briefly cooked vegetables, freshly squeezed juices and
mineral water are not recommended. Milk and dairy products are only
included in the diet if they don't cause problems. Don't use therapeutic
recipes over a longer period without consulting your doctor or therapist.

**Varied food**
Enjoy the diversity of foodstuffs. Characteristics of a balanced nutrition
are variety, suitable combination and a balanced quantity of rich and low
energy foodstuffs (on one hand avoiding undersupply with essential
nutrients and on the other hand to take to many undesirable substances).

## A lot of Cereal Products - and Potatoes

Bread, pasta, rice, cereal flakes (best wholemeal) as well as potatoes contain almost no fat, but many vitamins, mineral nutrients, trace elements, roughage and secondary plant substances. These foodstuffs ought to be taken with low-fat side dishes.

## Vegetables and Fruit – „Take Five" every day ...

5 portions of vegetables and fruit a day, as fresh as possible, briefly cooked, or maybe one portion as a juice – ideal as a side dish to every meal as well as snack between meals: Thus a lot of vitamins, mineral nutrients as well as roughage and secondary plant substances

## Daily milk and dairy products

Milk and Dairy Products every Day, once or twice per Week Fish; meat, sausages as well as eggs moderately. These foodstuffs contain valuable nutrients like calcium in the milk, iodine selenium and omega-3 fat acids in saltwater fish. Meat is favorable due to its high content of disposable iron and the vitamins B1, B6 and B12. Quantities of 300 – 600 g meat and sausage per week are sufficient. Prefer low-fat products, especially in meat- and dairy products.

## Low-fat and fatty Foodstuffs

Fat supplies us with essential fat acids and fatty foodstuffs contain also fat-soluble vitamins. Fat is high in energy; therefore much fat in the food may cause overweight, possibly also cancer. Too many saturated fat acids may further a tendency for cardio-vascular diseases in the long term. Prefer vegetable oils and fats (e.g. rapeseed-, olive-, soya-oils and solid fats produced therefrom). Beware of invisible fat in meat- and dairy products, pastry and sweets as well as in fast-food and convenience foods. 70 – 90 g fat per day is sufficient.

## Moderately Sugar and Salt

Take sugar and foods/drinks containing various kinds of sugar (e.g. glucose syrup) only occasionally. Use herbs and spices as well as a little salt creatively. Prefer salt containing iodine.

## Plenty of Liquids

Water is absolutely essential. Drink 1-2 l liquids every day. Prefer water (with or without gas) and other low-calorie drinks. Alcoholic drinks should not be taken.

**Tasty Dishes, carefully cooked**
Cook the meals with as low temperatures and as short as possible, using little water and fat – this preserves the original taste, keeps the nutrients intact and prevents the production of harmful compounds.

**Take time and enjoy the food**
Take your Time and enjoy your Food
Eating consciously helps to eat right. The eye enjoys food, too. It's fun, invites to enjoy varied dishes and stimulates the feeling of satiety.

**Watch your Weight and stay in Motion**
A balanced diet and a lot of exercise and sport (30 – 60 min/day) are a healthy combination. The right weight furthers well-being and health.
Thermals, directional effectiveness, digestive power
There are various criteria for judging the effectiveness of herbs and foodstuffs.
The use of certain herbs and ingredients is based on observations of the effects on the body which these foodstuffs, herbs and spices show after having eaten them. The medical science has developed following system: Every ingredient or herb has a directional effectiveness. Furthermore, there are herbs which have a special effect on certain organs.
The basic condition for a healthy metabolism is to obtain sufficient energy from food and that the digestive process doesn't use too much energy. An easily digestible meal makes content and sated, doesn't cause flatulence and fatigue after the meal. The perfect spices increase the healthiness of our meals. Very often, just small doses of herbs and spices will suffice. They are not used to make us sated, but to help our digestive organs to digest the food.


# 12.2 Recipes

The recipes list the ingredients to be used and the cooking instructions show how the dish is prepared. The list of ingredients shows the concerned quantities as well as the relevance for the therapy. If you find „less than mentioned", try to comply or find an alternative from the „list of recommended foodstuffs". Mostly it shall result just in a small change of taste when you simply avoid this ingredient.
Mild cooking methods: boiling, stewing, poaching, steaming
Strong cooking methods: barbecuing, roasting, frying, smoking
Balanced cooking methods: deep-frying, baking brick
Deep-freezing and warming in the microwave oven should be avoided (denaturalization).

## 12.3 Foodstuffs

Foodstuffs have an effect on body and soul like medicinal herbs, only a very much milder one. Dietary advice is mainly based on regional foodstuffs. The knowledge about the effects of each foodstuff and the knowledge, when which foodstuff shall be used, is based on the orthodoschool of medicine. Use ecologic-organic products, if possible. As everything should be cooked for a long time due to a better digestability and very rarely eaten raw, the food agrees with everyone.
The classification of the foodstuffs according to their effect on the body is the basis in order to achieve a harmonious status of health.
Dietary advisors do not recommend certain foodstuffs for everyone. The individual diet is tailor-made for the individual constitution.

Buy only fresh and ripe fruit and vegetables. You ought to leave unripe fruit and vegetables and such with brown spots and wilted leaves behind in the market. In this case take deep-frozen goods (never ready-to-serve dishes!). Fruit and vegetables are deep-frozen immediately after harvesting and often contain more vitamins and minerals than the goods from the vegetable shelf. Whereas conserved or tinned goods contain very much less biological substances. Also, salt, sugar and others are mostly added to the latter. Never leave the foodstuffs in the water after washing them to avoid that many vital substances get drowned. Clean salads, fruit and vegetables immediately before serving.

Please make sure of the hygienic processing of foodstuffs. Clean your salads, fruit and vegetables carefully. When cooking with meat, prepare all ingredients first and then process the meat products. Clean the worktop and tools very carefully. Wooden surfaces ought to be treated with a mild disinfectant regularly in order to reduce germination.
Store fruit and vegetables separately, if possible. Harvested fruit and vegetables are still alive and emit e.g. ethylene gas, which makes other products ripen and age faster. Keep meat and fish in the closed packaging or store them in the fridge in closed containers.

## 12.4 Herbs

There are some basic rules for storing medicinal herbs. On principle, herbs must be protected from direct sunlight, humidity and heat.

Containers for the storage of herbs may be glasses, ceramic jars and even plastic containers. However, plastic is a rather unsuitable material and should only be a short-term solution. In case of glass containers, use a dark material.

Medicinal herbs cannot be kept for any long period. The shelf life of herbs is limited. However, it can be prolonged with suitable storage. The place should be dark, rather cool and absolutely dry. A wooden medicine cabinet, placed not directly next to a source of heat, would be ideal. Never buy large quantities of herbs so as not to have to throw them away. Label the container with the name of the herb and the date of harvesting or processing.

# 13 Other dietic-books

The following syndromes of dietetics, TCM or for a therapy supplement for cancer are available.

## Dietetics

E001. Nutrition of the infant - baby food
E002. Nutrition during lactation
E003. Nutrition in old age
E004. Nutrition of children and adolescents
E005. Nutrition of athletes
E006. Light weight
E007. Pregnancy
E008. Full food

**Protein and electrolyte - kidneys**
E009. (hemodialysis) dialysis treatment
E010. Acute renal failure
E011. Chronic renal insufficiency
E012. Nephrotic syndrome
E013. Kidney stones (nephrolithiasis)

**Gastrointestinal tract - pancreas**
E014. Acute pancreatitis (inflammation of the pancreas)
E015. Chronic pancreatitis (inflammation of the pancreas)

**Gastrointestinal tract - small intestine and large intestine**
E016. Acute obstipation (constipation)
E017. Chronic obstipation (constipation)
E018. Colon irritabile
E019. Diverticulitis
E020. Acquired lactose intolerance (lactose malabsorption)
E021. Fructose malabsorption
E022. Glutensensitive enteropathy (celiac disease)
E023. Colectomy
E024. Short Bowel Syndrome

**Gastrointestinal tract - liver, gallbladder, bile ducts**

E025. Acute and chronic hepatitis (inflammation of the liver)
E026. Cholelithiasis (bile stones)
E027. fatty liver
E028. cirrhosis

**Gastrointestinal tract - Stomach and duodenal intestine**
E029. Acute gastritis
E030. Chronic gastritis
E031. Stomach bleeding
E032. Ulcus ventriculi and duodenal ulcer
E033. Condition after gastric surgery

**Gastrointestinal tract - oral cavity and esophagus**
E034. Stomatitis
E035. Esophageal carcinoma (esophageal cancer)
E036. Refluosophagitis (heartburn)

**Special diseases**
E037. Phenylketonuria (PKU)
E038. Rheumatic joint diseases

**Metabolism**
E039. Obesity (overweight)
E040. Diabetes mellitus
E041. Eating disorders (underweight)

**Fat metabolism**
E042. Hypercholesterolaemia (increased cholesterol level)
E043. Hepatic Encephalopathy

**Heart and circulation**
E044. Arteriosclerosis (arterial calcification)
E045. Heart insufficiency
E046. Hypertension
E047. Hyperuricaemia and gout

**Changed nutrient requirements**
E048. In case of fever
E049. For malignant diseases
E050. After burns
E051. Radiation and chemotherapy

# CANCER
E100. Pancreatic cancer
E101. Bladder cancer
E102. Blood cancer (leukemia)
E103. Breast cancer
E104. Colorectal cancer
E105. Gastric cancer
E106. Kidney cancer
E107. Esophageal cancer

E200. Bladder - moisture heat in the bladder
E201. Bladder - moisture and cold in the bladder
E202. Bladder - emptiness and cold in the bladder
E203. Large intestine - external cold affects the large intestine
E204. Large intestine - moisture heat in the large intestine
E205. Large intestine - heat blocks the intestine II acute
E206. Large intestine - dryness of the colon
E207. Large intestine - Yang deficiency (cold)
E208. Heart - Blood insufficiency
E209. Heart - Blood stagnation
E210. Heart - Fire
E211. Heart - Hot mucus clogs the heart pores
E212. Heart - Cold mucus clogs the heart pores
E213. Heart - Qi deficiency
E214. Heart - Yang deficiency
E215. Heart - Yin deficiency
E216. Liver - Ascending Liver Yang
E217. Liver - Blood deficiency
E218. Liver - Blood stagnation
E219. Liver - Moisture heat in liver and gall bladder
E220. Liver - Fire
E221. Liver - Gall bladder Qi-Empty
E222. Liver - Cold in the liver meridian
E223. Liver - Qi stagnation
E224. Liver - Wind
E225. Liver - Wind with ascending liver Yang
E226. Liver - Wind with blood anemic
E227. Liver - Wind with extreme heat
E228. Lung - Qi deficiency
E229. Lung - Mucus-moisture in the lungs
E230. Lung - Mucus-heat in the lungs
E231. Lung - Mucus-cold in the lungs
E232. Lung - Dryness of the lungs
E233. Lung - Wind-heat attacks the lungs
E234. Lung - Wind-cold affects the lungs
E235. Lung - Yin deficiency
E236. Stomach - Bloodstagnation
E237. Stomach - Fire
E238. Stomach - Cold with liquid
E239. Stomach - Nutrition stagnation
E240. Stomach - Qi deficiency
E241. Stomach - Rebellious Qi
E242. Stomach - Yin Emptiness
E243. Spleen - Heat and moisture attack the spleen
E244. Spleen - Coldness and moisture affects the spleen
E245. Spleen - Qi deficiency
E246. Spleen - Qi deficiency + Declining spleen Qi
E247. Spleen - Qi deficiency + spleen does not control the blood
E248. Spleen - Yang deficiency
E249. Kidney - Heart and kidney no longer communicate
E250. Kidney - Jing deficiency
E251. Kidney - Kidneys cannot receive the Qi
E252. Kidney - Qi is not stable

For further information visit nutribook.info.

# 14 EBNS - Software for nutritional counseling

The main task of the database is to create personalized nutritional advice for each patient individually. The database was developed for Dietetics and Traditional Chinese Medicine.
The Database supports training and advices in the daily work routine.

The computer program provides lists of recipes, ingredients and herbs, which are given to the client. individually adjustable according to patient's request from whole food to vegetarians (lacto, ovo, ...). For every register there is an information sheet which can be given to the client. All texts can be individually designed.

The syndromes can be combined and result in an intersection of the recommended recipes and ingredients. The automated diagnosis for the TCM enables you to check your experience during the training as well as to confirm your diagnosis in the working day. You select several predefined symptoms and have the program automatically display the relevant syndromes.

How to work with the database:
Select the patient / client, select one or more of the syndromes you diagnosed and print the folder.

You can change all values, create new symptoms or syndromes, develop recipes, change or adapt ingredients and herbs to your findings. In simple client management, all relevant data about the person is stored. You get an overview of the past diagnoses and the development of the course of the disease.

As a consultant you save a lot of time when you print out the recipe, food and herbal lists for the recognized syndromes and give them to the clients. You can use this time for a personal conversation. With the database, dieticians and nutritionists can view the nutrients and trace elements for each recipe and develop recipes for syndromes even with suggested ingredients.

All recipe and grocery lists can also be ordered from me as a combination of several diseases. I wish all readers good luck, health and happiness in life.

More information can be found at www.ebns.at.

Volunteer: www.krebsinfo.at

Josef Miligui